Children with Attentional Difficulties
A Guide for Teachers

What you need to know about that mADDening child

by Jack Crompton

Introduction

Every teacher needs to know about **A**ttention **D**eficit **D**isorder. Too often children with this condition have been excluded from school and/or consigned to residential establishments for those with emotional and behavioural difficulties. And yet, with the right combination of treatments and some thought given to structure within the classroom, these children are very often manageable in the mainstream school.

While a number of excellent books have been published on the subject in the last two or three years, they require a considerable commitment of time to read—a commitment which the hard-pressed modern teacher is usually unable to give. My aim, therefore, has been to produce something which can be read during one duty-free lunchtime, yet which can supply all the relevant facts, as we understand them at present, about this complex, stressful condition.

Jack Crompton

"Don't hate me! Help me!"

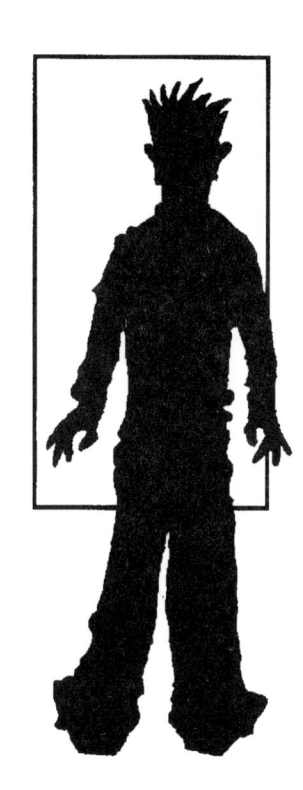

Is this another new bandwagon?

Most definitely not! The nature and causes of attentional difficulties have been under scrutiny throughout this century. The first written account we have actually dates back to the middle of the last century, but it was the British physician George Still's 1902 paper *Some Abnormal Psychical Conditions in Children* which brought focus to the condition. Interest in the way the brain influences behaviour increased after the great influenza pandemic, and the resultant encephalitis, at the end of World War I. The most recent advances in our understanding of attentional disorders have taken place in the USA.

To describe the condition as a **bandwagon** is to do a profound disservice to the very many people whose lives are affected by it—the sufferers themselves, their families, friends and colleagues, and their teachers.

Right, so what is it?

Attention Deficit Disorder is a medical condition which has been defined by the American Psychiatric Association. It is a lifelong condition, though the symptoms can change as the sufferer grows older, and also vary depending on the environment. It is probably inherited, as it certainly seems more prevalent in some families than in others. It is not influenced by the individual's intelligence.

ADD is caused by a malfunction of the neurotransmitters in the frontal lobe of the brain. These are chemicals released from nerve endings that transmit impulses from one neuron (nerve cell) to another, or to a muscle cell. The particular neurotransmitters concerned are those that regulate attention, impulsivity and motor activity.

It is a neurobiological disorder, it cannot be caused by inadequate parenting, poor housing, lead in the air, chemicals in food or any other environmental factors.

The condition manifests itself in one or more of the following areas:

    a) sustaining attention

    b) controlling impulsivity

    c) controlling motor activity

The condition is chronic and persistent. Typically, symptoms start to become obvious around 3 to 4 years (when the child is expected to have learnt certain behaviours) and will be seen in a variety of situations. A child with ADD will have trouble paying attention and concentrating. He will be easily distracted by outside events, but will also daydream.

Where hyperactivity is present (Attention Deficit/Hyperactivity Disorder), the symptoms are even more apparent, with disruptive and destructive behaviour causing difficulties at home and at school.

A child with ADD cannot learn appropriate behaviour. He makes no connection between a particular pattern of behaviour and its consequences. If you point out his mistakes to him, he may acknowledge them and be very sorry for what he has done, but this will not stop him from doing the same thing again a few minutes later. Neither punishment nor rewards seem to affect his behaviour. He is truly a mADDening child!

How common is Attention Deficit Disorder?

Figures quoted range from 0.5% to 6% of the school population, the lower estimates occurring for the UK, the higher ones for the USA. There is no doubt that the condition has been significantly underdiagnosed in this country. This is because the medical profession here has tended to adhere to the World Health Organisation's definition of 'hyperkinetic syndrome', which covers only those cases where hyperactivity is present. If we say that around 3% of children may suffer from ADD, this is probably a reasonably accurate estimate. This, of course, does not mean that 3% of the children in **your** school must necessarily have the condition.

Research shows that in around half of the cases ADD continues to pose significant problems in adulthood.

Is it really serious?

Yes. ADD is just as real a disability as sensory impairment, autism or physical handicap. But, being 'invisible', it provokes a less than sympathetic reaction. The picture I have painted so far may seem simple, but in reality it is never so.

Characteristics of the disorder range from mild to severe, and the symptoms themselves vary from individual to individual. There is no such person as 'the ADD child', and such labelling is unhelpful. Further, ADD can occur in conjunction with other difficulties, such as specific learning disabilities and speech and language problems; or with other neurological conditions and juvenile psychiatric disorders.

Where ADD remains untreated, complications soon start to occur. Even before the child begins school he will have already suffered stress due to his condition. He is likely to have been told off, snapped at and punished to no avail. The parents' relationship may have become fragile as a consequence of the strained atmosphere at home. Because of constant criticism, the child's concept of self-worth may be low. When meeting a new set of adults, his teachers, whose behavioural expectations he has no chance of meeting, his low self-esteem may be reinforced, reducing his confidence to make friends. Indeed, his peers may soon realise that contact with him can lead to getting hurt or getting into trouble.

Disaffection from school develops during the primary years: the youngster becomes argumentative and defiant, or he withdraws into himself. Lacking social skills, he is aggressive towards his peers, or he deliberately shuns them. He earns a bad reputation. He is labelled 'slow', 'lazy', 'unmotivated', 'naughty', 'disruptive', 'a pest'.

At secondary school, punishment in place of understanding can only make the situation worse. All too often the young person engages in persistent challenging behaviour, truants, gets in with 'the wrong crowd', and may become involved in petty thieving and substance abuse.

In adulthood, ADD can cause such problems as an inability to form and maintain relationships, or hold down a job; drug addiction; depression; alcoholism, and criminal activities.

Is that serious enough?

Yes! You'd better tell me how we can recognise ADD in school

Where the hyperactivity component is present, the child will stand out in a very obvious way. Other sufferers may be less easy to detect: their listlessness and poor concentration may simply be dismissed as laziness.

A child with ADD will exhibit many of the following characteristics to a degree and with a frequency well in excess of his classmates.

Inattentiveness:

- fails to finish work
- seems not to listen, does not follow instructions
- is easily distracted, has short attention span
- cannot concentrate on tasks
- is disorganised, work looks a mess, does not bring P.E. kit or writing equipment, loses things
- forgets things quickly
- daydreams, seems oblivious of what is going on
- hands in homework late, or not at all
- puts off starting tasks
- makes careless mistakes

Impulsivity:

- flits between different activities, never finishing one
- acts or speaks without thinking, calls out, answers questions before they are finished
- cannot wait turn in groupwork, games or line
- is clumsy/accident-prone, breaks things, accidentally hurts others
- cannot sit and listen to a story
- makes remarks inappropriate to the situation

Hyperactivity:

- is 'out of control' or 'on the go'
- throws tantrums
- runs about room, climbs on furniture
- cannot sit still or stay in one place
- demands attention
- fidgets, fiddles, squirms, taps, pokes, kicks
- is talkative and noisy

Shared Characteristics:

- seems not to learn what is appropriate or inappropriate through rewards or punishment, and is unable to take advantage of behaviour management techniques, positive reinforcement or 'talk therapy'
- is negative about own self-worth, says 'I can't do that' before trying, keeps restarting work or screws it up
- is making little progress
- underachieves, shows verbal skills superior to anything that appears on paper
- tries to be class clown
- avoids eye contact

- is much better with individual attention
- seems immature
- is bossy in games, and cannot share or take turns
- has few friends, is aggressive
- tests out rules and structures

The above gives a profile of what a child with ADD may be like. Some of the characteristics are mutually exclusive, and not all will be present in one individual. Please do not try to use the above as a checklist; diagnostic criteria (known as DSM IV) have been produced by the American Psychiatric Association and can be found in some of the publications I list at the end of this booklet. There are also a number of behaviour rating scales available which can be used by teachers.

Most of the children I teach seem to be suffering from this as well as half the staff

Right—you're making an important point. Any of us can be inattentive, impatient or overactive at times. But someone with ADD is like this most of the time. Also, a lot of the above can be symptoms of behavioural difficulties caused by environmental factors, such as inappropriate work being set in school or some sort of major disturbance at home. Some of the characteristics are similar to those shown by children with a specific learning disability. Or there may be another medical explanation for the behaviour, such as Asperger Syndrome or epilepsy. Often there is a combination of factors causing the behaviour.

Ask the following questions:

➡ Has the behaviour been going on for at least six months?

➡ Did it start before the age of seven?

➡ Are most of the symptoms, as defined by the APA, present?

➡ Is the behaviour causing problems in all areas of the child's life—at home and in the neighbourhood, as well as at school?

➡ Is the behaviour seriously hindering his educational and social development?

If you cannot answer 'yes' to all of these questions, you are unlikely to be dealing with ADD.

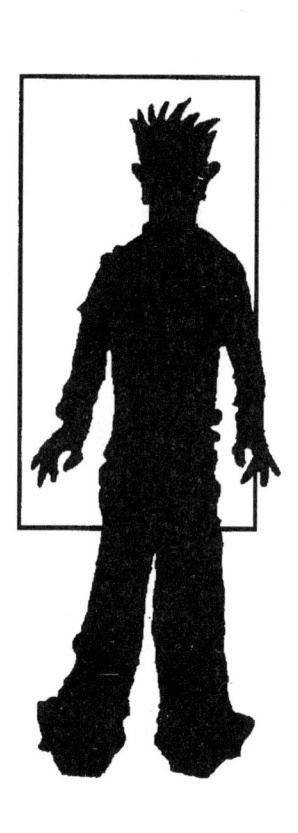

By the way, I notice you keep saying 'he' and 'his'

That's right. The condition is far more likely to be diagnosed in boys than in girls. One explanation is that ADD is passed down the male side of the family. But it is almost certainly the case that ADD is underdiagnosed in girls. Hyperactive and aggressive behaviour has a higher profile than inattentive behaviour, and is more frequently seen in boys than in girls. My concern is that those children, boys as well as girls, suffering from 'classic' (undifferentiated) ADD may tend to be overlooked, as hyperactivity is more easily identifiable. It is also unfortunate that, since DSM IV, the leading professionals in the field refer almost exclusively to ADHD, as if hyperactivity is an essential component of the condition. I don't want the quiet, withdrawn daydreamers to be forgotten.

Can ADD be cured?

Although there is no known cure for the condition, it can be brought under control, and the youngster can learn to live more comfortably with it. Real progress, however, depends on everyone working together—teachers, parents, psychologists and medical practitioners.

There is no proven medical test which will identify ADD, although positron emission tomography scans are used successfully in research into the condition and may soon become a regular diagnostic tool. At present, assessment is a complex and lengthy process. Diagnosis itself can be made only by a physician. As few family doctors are well enough informed about the disorder, this in effect means involving a consultant paediatrician or a consultant child/ adolescent psychiatrist. A complicating factor is usually that ADD coexists with other problems.

To form a precise picture of the child's difficulties, it is essential, therefore, to obtain information from as many sources as possible. Obviously, the school has a major role to play here. The child is likely to be on the school's SEN register, and IEPs, detailed observations and reports will prove invaluable. Information from the educational psychologist, doctor, family members and anyone else able to offer a view of the child will be gathered in order to build up an accurate profile. A battery of medical and psychological tests will be carried out. As you can see, this is a team effort, and teachers have an important part to play as educational experts.

This 'multi-modal' approach is also necessary in the treatment of ADD, and the school needs to make sure that it is involved in any discussion of educational provision, as well as being informed about the psychological and medical aspects of the treatment.

The needs of individual children vary, but it is unlikely that learning can be enhanced or a significant level of normality be brought to the sufferer's life, without the use of a combination of approaches. If the child is to remain in mainstream education, he will probably require additional support: this usually comes through a statement of special educational needs. At the very least, the school will require advice in devising modified teaching programmes.

The child is also likely to require help in raising self-esteem, developing social skills and learning appropriate behaviour through rules, routines and positive reinforcement. Counselling and other forms of therapy, if necessary, should be accessed through educational psychologists or other support agencies.

A strong element of liaison will need to exist between school and home. Quite often, relationships between the two will have been rocky, and trust will have to be built up. The family itself may require therapy and training.

Medically, the condition will usually be controlled through the prescription of an appropriate drug. This provides the 'breathing space' the child needs in order to be able to start learning, and living a normal life.

Tell me about the drugs. Are they necessary? Are they safe? What do they actually do?

Let me reiterate that no single approach will bring results by itself. Giving a child medicine and then putting him back into an unstructured, stressful home situation, or into a classroom where he will be shouted at and punished for every wrong move, will not lead to any significant progress.

The purpose of medication is to stimulate levels of chemical activity in the frontal lobe of the brain, thus enhancing the message-carrying capabilities of the neurotransmitters. Note that these are stimulants, not tranquillisers—media talk of a 'chemical cosh' or 'Prozac for kids' is therefore ignorant as well as irresponsible.

Medication therapy has been in use since the 1930s. There are two main groups of drugs: psychostimulants, of which Ritalin (medical name methylphenidate) is the best known, and anti-depressants such as Tofranil (imipramine). Ritalin has been in regular use for nearly 50 years and has an excellent safety record. Possible side effects include sleeplessness, loss of appetite and feelings of nausea, but these can usually be corrected by adjusting the dose. Despite scare stories, the taking of such medication does not lead to drug dependency. ADD untreated often leads to drug addiction in adolescence and adulthood. Conversely, studies have shown that young people who take Ritalin will consciously try to adjust the dose downwards when they feel ready.

Medication is successful in around 80% of cases: that is, symptoms of inattentiveness, impulsivity and hyperactivity are significantly reduced. This can happen quickly and dramatically if the dosage is correct. Ritalin begins to work within 15-20 minutes and the effects last for 3-4 hours. Where medication is less successful in modifying behaviour, this is probably due to the severity of concomitant problems.

Medication helps the sufferer to help himself. It does not control him. If anything, it helps him learn self-control through his own efforts, supported by a package of other treatment strategies. The child and his family do, of course, have the right to reject medication.

What can we do to help in school?

First, let me ask **you** a couple of questions. Is the ethos of your school positive and caring? If responsibility is taken for the educational well-being of **all** children, whatever challenges they present, there is a good chance of progress. If you're not sure about this, a quick look at your school's exclusion rates will give you a rough idea.

The second question is directed at you personally. Will your beliefs permit you to work in a positive way with this child? You need to accept that ADD is a real disability, and not naughtiness on the part of the child, which he could stop if he really wanted to. You must also accept that behavioural difficulties can sometimes have a biological cause. This could be a problem for you if you have been trained in a sociological/behavourist approach, which will admit only of environmental reasons for behaviour. If you are to help the child with ADD, you will need to move your beliefs on and accept the possibility that other factors can be involved.

Children with attention deficits need routine and structure more than most. They also need to start achieving personal success, in the first place by building on those strengths which they do have. Most importantly, they need to be in a calm, accepting and sympathetic environment.

A whole-school approach

Everyone on the teaching and ancillary staff needs to be aware of what ADD is and how the children involved are being treated. Everyone needs to be doing and saying the same things, and any differences of opinion need to be aired and resolved at the outset. Attempts to teach children with ADD through an undifferentiated curricular approach are unlikely to be successful, and will cause stress in the teachers as well as in the children.

Classroom structure

The classroom should be self-contained and not used as a thoroughfare. The child should be seated near the front of the class or near the teacher's desk, away from windows and doors. Ideally, there will be a curriculum access assistant to give the child some individual attention, or to oversee the other children while the teacher works with him. Simple routines should be established—e.g. for entering and leaving the room, for starting work, for changing activities. A few basic rules should be displayed clearly in the classroom, together with their positive and negative consequences. Pair the child with one who is successful and well-motivated: this will be more productive in the early stages than plunging him straight into a group.

Tackling inattentiveness

Instruction should be simple, with no sub-parts, and broken down into small steps. Get the child to repeat them to you. Make an individual work programme that he can fasten to his desk, and colour in or tick off tasks as he completes them.

Monitor the child's attention span and set tasks to fit this, with a reward at the end of each. Gradually develop the attention span as the child succeeds. At the end of a piece of desk work, allow a short physical activity (e.g. taking a message, sorting crayons). Be with the child at the start of the task to explain it, then check back regularly. Speak often to him, using his name and making eye contact. When redirecting back on to task, be specific:

> ' Paul, you're working on maths card number 5,'
> **not**
> ' Get on with your work.'

If the child needs extra time to complete a task, give him this without any criticism. Finally, be aware that his attentiveness will lessen as the medication wears off, so arrange tasks with this in mind.

Changing behaviour

Concentrate on one unacceptable behaviour at a time and aim to replace it with one that is positively phrased. Set him achievable targets, based on your previously recorded observations, and make sure that any rewards built into the programme will be meaningful to him.

Raising self-esteem and developing a sense of responsibility

Make sure the child has prompt, positive feedback on the completion of each task. Encourage him to evaluate his own achievements. Build on his strengths: he may have practical, artistic or sporting skills that can be developed. Find out what interests him and let him do project work on that subject. Work with him on coping with challenging situations and controlling his temper—help him to develop assertiveness skills. Allow him to remove himself quietly to 'time out' when he feels the pressure growing too much. Give him responsibilities within the classroom, and also make him responsible for taking his medicine. If feasible, set up a 'circle of friends' for him.

Working with parents

Having the family on your side is half the battle. Up to now they may only have had bad news from school. Hopefully, they should soon be receiving positive messages. Set up regular meetings with parents to discuss progress and setbacks. Exchange information: find out how they are coping at home, and make sure they tell you of any changes in dosage or type of medication. Make sure they understand what the school policy is and how it is being implemented in your classroom. Where homework completion is a problem, advise on establishing good study habits. If you can't meet regularly because of their work commitments, arrange a time when you can telephone.

All of this may not be specific enough for your own situation. You can, however, seek out relevant 'on-the-spot' advice from the school's psychologist and other support services.

What else do I need to know?

It is worth bearing in mind that ADD **does** have some positive characteristics. For instance, in the right situation, people with the condition display great persistence and determination, tremendous energy, acute observational skills, inquisitiveness, divergent and creative thinking processes, sensitivity and a willingness to take risks. If you can see the child with ADD in this way, rather than as a collection of deficits, you will be helping to boost his self-esteem, as well as feeling more positive yourself.

Cooper and Ideus (1996) illustrate a reframing technique which you may find useful. This takes a negative characteristic and rephrases it in a positive way: e.g. 'he talks out of turn' becomes 'he's keen to contribute'.

That sounds like a promising approach. I'm keen to find out more now.

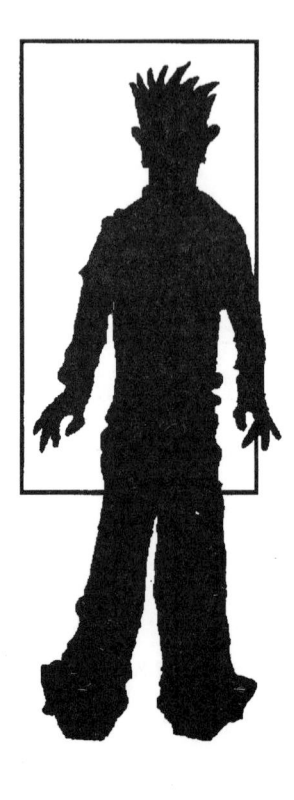

Where should I look?

For a start, you could contact LADDER—the National Learning and Attention Deficit Disorders Association. For information and membership details write to them at P.O. Box 700, Wolverhampton WV3 7YY, or telephone (O1902) 336272,

You could direct concerned parents towards LADDER, and also to the ADD/ADHD Family Support Group at 1a. The High Street, Dilton Marsh, Westbury BA13 4DL, telephone (01373) 826045. The quotation at the beginning of this booklet is the group's motto.

Relevant books, videos and audio tapes are available from:
ADD Information Services, P.O. Box 340, Edgware HA8 9HL
Telephone (0181) 9052013.

Further Reading

I would like to recommend three books which I have found very useful.

Sheppard, A (1995)
Attention Deficit Disorder
Available from First & Best in Education Ltd, 34 Nene Valley Business Park, Oundle, Peterborough PE8 4HL.
An accessible, clearly written account of the subject, aimed at teachers, and with plenty of practical advice.

Cooper, P & Ideus, K (1996)
Attention Deficit/Hyperactivity Disorder: a practical guide for teachers.
London, David Fulton.
Packed with information from the latest research, written to provoke self-questioning in the reader. Would make a good basis for INSET.

Cooper, P & Ideus, K (ed. 1995)
Attention Deficit/Hyperactivity Disorder: educational medical and cultural issues.
East Sutton, Association of Workers for Children with Emotional and Behavioural Difficulties.
Explores the research, mainly American, and presents it for a UK readership.

Finally, the quarterly journal *Emotional and Behavioural Difficulties* frequently contains articles on ADD.